Paris: Made by Hand

PARIS: MADE BY HAND

Pia Jane Bijkerk

THE LITTLE BOOKROOM
New York

©2009 The Little Bookroom
©2009 Pia Jane Bijkerk
Photographs ©2009 by Pia Jane Bijkerk

Cover design and photograph: Pia Jane Bijkerk
Book design: Laura-Jane Coats
Book production: Adam Hess

Bijkerk, Pia.
 Made by hand / text and photographs by Pia Bijkerk.
    p. cm.
 Includes index.
 ISBN 978-1-892145-70-3 (alk. paper)
 1. Handicraft—France—Paris—Guidebooks. 2. Artisans—
France—Paris—Guidebooks. I. Title.
 TT72.P37 2009
 745.50944'361—dc22

                         2008040201

Published by The Little Bookroom
435 Hudson St., 3rd floor
New York, NY 10014
www.littlebookroom.com
editorial@littlebookroom.com

10 9 8 7 6 5 4 3

Printed in China

For Mum and Dad

Pour Romain

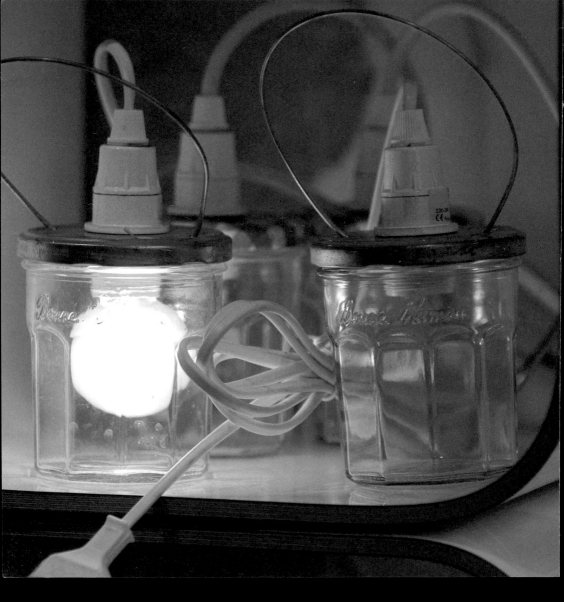

CONTENTS

◆

S A STYLIST, I AM ALWAYS ON THE LOOKOUT FOR OBJECTS THAT ARE DISTINCTIVE AND ALLURING—WHICH IS WHY I ADORE ALL THINGS handmade. And Paris just happens to be a rather wonderful place to find the things I adore.

A designer's muse, a decorator's heaven, and a treasure trove for a stylist: Paris may very well be one of the last remaining international cities that strives to protect and nurture her artisans. Restored buildings are frequently appointed to house workshops and studios, and a growing number of shops are devoted to exhibiting the works of Parisian artists and craftspeople. Although mass-produced products have dominated those made by hand in modern times, Paris loyally and lovingly upholds its traditions. All things handmade, or *fait main* in French, therefore remain at the heart of Paris. And in this *belle époque*, as we grow weary of the sameness of mass-production, *fait main* takes center stage once again.

Paris: Made by Hand is an insider's look at the city's artisans, *créateurs*, and crafts boutiques. You'll discover some *ateliers* that have been around for hundreds of years (many of which are tucked into the oldest of *passages* or hidden courtyards), and others that have just surfaced. Between the pages of this guide you can expect to find papermakers, shoemakers, jewelry designers, milliners, umbrella makers, dressmakers, ceramicists, and more: All of them from my private little black book, and all of them right in the heart of the city. Among them you'll discover an exquisite, century-old haberdashery that I go to when I need ribbon and silk from a by-gone era, and a boutique, in the hub of Le Marais, that is *the* place for finding new handcrafted designer housewares.

And note: *Fait main* is not just about creating a new object by hand. Here, the concept also includes the act of restyling, restoring, or reinterpreting a found object, thereby giving it a new life and a new function. In French, the act of finding vintage objects has its own verb· *chiner*. And *chineurs* are the talented individuals who *chinent*. Many of the *chineurs* I have included in this book have the ability to see a found object in a whole new light, and they can't wait to get back to the studio and get their hands dirty—polishing, sanding, painting, or varnishing. Whether it has been simply restored or completely re-created, once finished, the article now bears a new handprint. The piece has been resurrected into a new era, ready to find a new home.

In this book I guide you from one trove to the next, and from one *arrondissement* to another, yet not with the intention to reveal all. While you wander between stops, you will spot other treasures along the way, allowing you to create your own *fait main* tour.

As we all know, sometimes the French have a way of saying things that just can't be better described in any other language. In other words, there are certain things that just sound more beautiful *en français*. So to get you started, here is a brief glossary of terms to pack in your suitcase before you set out on this new adventure:

Atelier: studio/workshop

Bricoler: to make/do/adjust/repair things with your hands (DIY, or Do-It-Yourself)

Bricoleur: the person who enjoys bricoler

Brocantes: flea markets

Chineur: someone who finds antiques and old things

Créateur: designer

Fait main: made by hand

Mercerie: boutique selling sewing and craft supplies

Paris, darling, it's my greatest pleasure to draw back your red velvet curtains and show everyone what is going on backstage. It's time to expose your true beauty, the one that lies within.

PIA JANE BIJKERK

WANDER

1

The First & Second Arrondissements

WANDER

① 1

T HE FIRST AND SECOND *ARRONDISSEMENTS* ARE FILLED WITH *FAIT MAIN* SHOPS—SOME WELL KNOWN, SOME CENTURIES OLD, AND SOME simply quaint, hidden-away treasures. Even though this is the most expensive part of Paris, there are still craftspeople to be found, busily working in the studios at the back of their boutiques. Starting at *métro* Châtelet and ending at the Quatre Septembre station, this wander will take you from one handmade delight to the next. Don't forget to keep your head up and eyes open as you walk from one to the other, as there is plenty of *fait main* inspiration along the way, and you will not want to miss a thing.

LA DROGUERIE

9-11, rue du Jour

1ᵉ ARRONDISSEMENT ~ MÉTRO Châtelet

TÉLÉPHONE 01 45 08 93 27

Monday ~ 2:30 to 6:45pm, Tuesday through Saturday ~ 10:30am to 6:45pm

www.ladroguerie.com

L A DROGUERIE OPENED IN THE 1970S, WHEN IT WAS DIFFI-
CULT TO FIND QUALITY SUPPLIES FOR DRESSMAKING AND
sewing. Now, what was once a butcher's shop is a craft
boutique, and a world-renowned one at that. The shop is a
destination not just for those interested in crafts, but for
those seeking ambience, too. When you enter the elongated
space you are greeted by skeins of luscious wool hanging
from the old butcher hooks and lined up like cotton candy.
There are dozens of little wooden drawers piled with buttons, baskets full of variously sized knitting needles, and
shelves of colored beads in plump glass jars with silver
punch ladles for scooping. There are ribbons made in
France, feathers, twine, and spools and spools of thread
(ninety colors to be exact). The list goes on.

The family who runs the business has seen a distinct trend
in recent years toward customizing garments and items
bought from large chain stores. Their business is well
stocked with all the necessities to do so.

feuille de ginkgo
0,50
feuille de trèfle
0,40

ASTIER DE VILLATTE

173, rue St-Honoré
1" ARRONDISSEMENT ~ MÉTRO Palais Royal
TÉLÉPHONE 01 42 60 74 13
Monday through Saturday • 11am to 7:30pm
www.astierdevillatte.com

A *TROUVAILLE* OF *FAIT MAIN* WARES, ASTIER DE VILLATTE SITS INCONSPICUOUSLY ON THIS FASHION-CONSCIOUS street. The building was once occupied by a silver-smith to Napoleon. Two hundred years later, the antique rooms, with their heavily timeworn ambience, are again filled with all things handmade. Most are crafted in Paris and designed by co-founders Ivan Pericoli and Benoît Astier de Villatte; the shop also displays the work of Parisian artist Nathalie Lété, whose whimsical and dainty white ceramics are so popular that the boutique now distributes the collection throughout the world. An entire room in the back of the premises, once the silversmith's workshop, is dedicated to her collection. I like to sneak in here each time I am on this famous *rue*, and purchase a Nathalie Lété piece for my prop collection—her divine dishes always come in handy for shoots.

Upstairs is an Alice-in-Wonderland-style showroom, with the walls covered in cherry-red and gold embossed wallpaper. The room is small, and the ceiling feels as if it is lowering as you walk farther into the space. The furnishings change regularly, but the room somehow retains a magical

and mysterious atmosphere. Head down ancient stone steps to the basement to find more exquisite furniture created by the Astier de Villatte team. It's another unusual space: grottolike, but with very contemporary tables, chairs, and cabinets. Somehow, it all works.

Also among the ever-changing collections at Astier de Villatte are glasses, cutlery, jewelry, vintage knickknacks, paper products, and hand-printed fabrics. It's eclectic, impressive, and ever inspiring.

ALEXIA HOLLINGER

3, rue Thérèse

1ˢᵗ ARRONDISSEMENT ~ MÉTRO Pyramides

TÉLÉPHONE 01 42 60 99 11

Tuesday through Friday ~ noon to 7:30pm

http://www.alexiahollinger.com

ALEXIA HOLLINGER IS AN ARTISAN WHO TRANSFORMS VINTAGE TEXTILES INTO EXQUISITE HANDBAGS THAT ARE suitably sophisticated for the streets of this ultra-chic city. Her boutique-*atelier* is set in idyllic rue Thérèse, just a stone's throw from the Palais Royal.

When Hollinger opened the boutique thirteen years ago she was struck by the haughty mindset of those who were not interested in buying bags if they were not made from leather; it seemed that fabric bags were just not part of Parisian fashion culture. But her impeccable craftsmanship and unique choice of textiles soon won a devoted following. Hollinger sources many of her materials from *brocantes* and uses vintage silk scarves to create one-of-a-kind purses. She also makes collections in new fabrics, creating stories and themes to suit different seasons and fashion trends. (Note: If you happen to be looking for that exquisite blue and red number on this page, I'm sorry, but I snapped it up for myself.)

All styles are fitted with inner pockets, phone holders, and key rings. Prices range from 65€ to 150€ for the one-off, vintage silk bags.

LEGERON

20, rue des Petits-Champs
2nd ARRONDISSEMENT ~ MÉTRO Pyramides
TÉLÉPHONE 01 42 96 94 89
By appointment
www.legeron.com

A VISIT TO LEGERON MIGHT SEEM A BIT DAUNTING. NOT ONLY MUST YOU CLIMB FIVE FLIGHTS OF CREAKING wooden stairs to reach the *atelier*, you may well end up brushing shoulders with a designer from the house of Lacroix, Ungaro, or Dior as you pass in the narrow stairwell. But be assured that Monsieur Legeron is very welcoming and will guide you, perhaps while whistling a tune, down a dark corridor to a showroom where you can see and touch the thousands of fabric blossoms made at Legeron. Here, in a workshop that appears not to have noticed the coming and going of the twentieth century, *haute couture* is nurtured; designers come to discuss and embellish upcoming collections with Monsieur Legeron.

The *atelier* is on the premises, just behind the thick walls of the showroom. It is buzzing with activity—petals are being shaped by hand, feathers are being dyed, tiny black blooms are hanging to dry on dainty pegs, and bottles of vibrant dyes wait to be opened by the artisan's heavily stained fingertips. The company was founded in 1880; Monsieur Legeron is the great-grandson of the founder and has a wonderful collection of old photos to show if you are interested in

LEGERON

Legeron history. Prices befit the prestige of Monsieur Legeron's main clients. However, you can still find an exquisite flower starting at about 40€, although large orders are preferred and wedding orders are quite welcome.

As at Maison Legeron, you can feel the rich history attached to the premises. The shop itself is split into two boutiques situated directly opposite each other—one dedicated to hats and hat accessories, and the other to sewing supplies. This is a special place where you'll want to take your time and search through every nook and cranny.

WANDER

2

The Third & Eleventh Arrondissements

WANDER

2

ELCOME TO THE HIP, HAPPENING, ARTSY QUARTER KNOWN AS LE MARAIS, SPREAD BETWEEN THE THIRD AND FOURTH *ARRONDISSE-ments* on the left and right banks of the River Seine. Set the scene by starting at the marvelously crafted *métro* station Arts et Métiers, then stroll through some of the mazelike backstreets to discover these *arrondissements'* secret *fait main* treasures. Detour a little into the neighboring eleventh *arrondissement* to the den of an interior designer who restores and reuses salvaged pieces, then step back into the third to a distinguished designer's inspiring haven. And while you are here, and you'd like to visit a true Parisian institution, visit the huge BHV, the Bazar de l'Hotel de Ville (14, rue du Temple, fourth arrondissement) a destination for all lovers of home decorating and refurbishment, with an entire floor dedicated to art and craft supplies, and a basement full of DIY paraphernalia.

PEP'S

Passage de l'Ancre Royal

(Entrances: 223, rue St-Martin and rue de Turbigo)

3ʳᵈ ARRONDISSEMENT ~ MÉTRO Arts et Métiers

TÉLÉPHONE 01 42 78 11 67

Monday through Thursday ~ 1:30 to 7pm, Saturday ~ 9am to 12:30pm

(September to May), Friday by appointment

www.peps-paris.com

I T MIGHT SEEM STRANGE TO EXPECT AN UMBRELLA REPAIR SHOP TO BE INTERESTING OR FASHIONABLE. BUT THIS IS PARIS, where repairs, alterations, craftsmanship, and restoration services have never ceased to be appreciated. The Marais, the *quartier du parapluie* (umbrella quarter), is home to one of the most popular repair shops in the city, proving that mending umbrellas is indeed a bustling trade.

Pep's is situated in Passage de l'Ancre Royal, Paris' oldest arcade. Step through the worn wooden doorway to this cobbled and alleyway, lovingly maintained and clad in overgrown ivy. This incredible walkway will take you back four hundred years, although Pep's is not so ancient.

Thierry Millet is the new "Pep," having acquired the forty-year-old establishment in 2003. The moment Thierry opens the doors at 1:30 on weekday afternoons the pocket-sized shop front receives a nonstop stream of customers from all over the country and abroad. It's a lively one-stop shop, with customers bringing in antique parasols, picking up repaired umbrellas, or coming to cast an eye over Millet's ready-made selection. Telescopic bumbershoots start around 45€, with non-telescopics starting around 70€ and working their way up to 150€. And just like old times, Pep does not take credit cards, so arm yourself with euros before you head his way.

MARIE LOUISE DE MONTEREY

1, rue Charles François Dupuis
3rd ARRONDISSEMENT ~ MÉTRO Temple
TÉLÉPHONE 01 48 04 83 88
Tuesday through Saturday + noon to 7pm
marielouisedemonterey.com

I T IS WORTH MEANDERING OFF THE WELL-WALKED STREETS OF THIS TRENDY QUARTER TO FIND MARIE LOUISE DE Monterey, tucked away on one of the Marais' quiet back *ruelles*. The shop guards a cache of classic vintage frocks, dainty blouses, and vintage children's wear, all hand chosen by owner Maria Vrisakis. Think timeless, romantic, unique, and oh-so-Parisian. Maria sources all her garments from *brocantes* and restores them to their former glory before placing them into the collection. A soft cotton cream blouse with lace cuffs might be 40€, while a hand stitched 1920s Paris evening slip is priced at around 200€. Among the regular clientele are actresses looking for (and happily finding) their red carpet dresses for the Cannes Film Festival. Chic French frocks are certainly Maria's best sellers—you may find a 1990s drop waisted rust-colored silk dress with velvet flowers on the hem, or a 1940s black empire-line evening gown with cap sleeves and coral beading on the shoulders. Although not bound to name brands only, the proprietress does keep a lookout for classic Yves Saint Laurent numbers and changes her stock seasonally. She shares her boutique with the vintage-inspired fashion label Lyell. It's a perfect match.

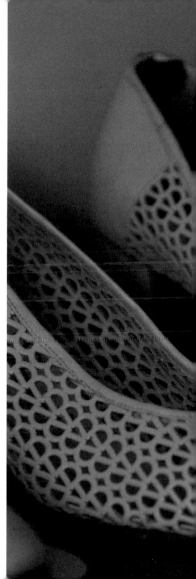

LES CURIEUSES

4, rue Oberkampf

11th ARRONDISSEMENT ~ MÉTRO St-Sébastien Froissart

TÉLÉPHONE 01 47 00 97 65

Tuesday through Saturday • 10:30am to 2pm and 3 to 7:30pm

www.lescurieuses.com

SLIGHT DETOUR FROM LE MARAIS INTO THE NEIGHBOR-
ING 11TH *ARRONDISSEMENT* WILL LEAD YOU TO ANOTHER
creative haven frequented by the interior designers
and stylists of Paris.

Architectural associates David Gaillard and Bruno Tin
opened Les Curieuses in 2007. This creative space on lively rue Oberkampf is an *atelier* and a showroom in which the
duo design and display furniture for their clients. The loca-
tion dates back to the nineteenth century and is one of the
rare Parisian boutiques that remain unchanged. David and
Bruno prefer to retain the architectural framework and have
brought only a touch of the modern to the space.

Restoration and reuse of salvaged pieces is very much a part
of Parisian culture, so it is not surprising that Gaillard and
Tin also source many of their pieces from *brocantes* found
throughout the Paris suburbs. They also offer a tasteful
selection of home furnishings and housewares.

In the main boutique the pair have shown handcrafted polished metal chairs with a sleek wrought-iron and wood-
topped dining table (the table is set with dishes with chubby

rims on slate placemats). An Estelle Lemaître light shade (see page 183) with spotted-feather trim hangs over the arrangement. Lemaître and the partners at Les Curieuses are friends and often work together on the same interior design project.

Beyond the *atelier* and office, and up the narrow staircase, is a showroom set up like a Parisian apartment. It's inviting and full of old French charm with a modern twist. A soft handwoven shawl is draped over a restored vintage arm-chair. A sleek lined lounge fitted with a simple black linen slipcover is a tempting place to curl up for a respite.

THE COLLECTION

has a vast selection of limited-edition designer wall stickers that can be adapted to your space or made to order. The staff is very helpful and always willing to brainstorm your latest interior design dilemmas. Prices range from 10€ to 800€.

WANDER

3

The Fourth Arrondissement

MÉLODIES GRAPHIQUES
- 63 -

PAPIER PLUS
- 67 -

KANEA
- 71 -

WANDER

3

THE FOURTH *ARRONDISSEMENT* IS UNDENIABLY ROMANTIC. STROLLING THROUGH IT, CROSSING OVER ONE OF THE PICTURESQUE BRIDGES, and gazing out over the Seine leaves one starry eyed. There is one quiet little *rue* in these parts for devotees of all things *fait main*. Follow a narrow back street from the *métro* Saint Paul to rue du Pont Louis-Philippe to discover a charming selection of stationery boutiques. Once you have replenished your paper supplies, pop around the corner for a cup of tea and cake at Ebouillante, a sun-drenched café that also serves a scrumptious Sunday brunch. Then pick up where you left off and slowly meander along rue du Pont Louis-Philippe onto the *pont* itself, over the Ile Saint-Louis, and across the second bridge that leads you straight to Notre Dame. After this enchanting stroll, chances are you will never suffer from *l'angoisse de la page blanche* (writer's block) again.

type. It takes him about three minutes to complete one envelope.

Quills start at 1.5€, inks are around 6€, and handmade notepads are priced about 10€ and up. Before you round up your goodies on the counter, check the scribbled pages of the open notebook near the quills in the center display—some years ago Monsieur Detugny discovered that his store was more than just a place for stationery lovers: a mysterious and torrid romance was being played out right in his boutique, with the couple leaving secret messages for each other in this notebook, including times and places to meet. Check the open page; you never know, there may be a message there for you.

PAPIER PLUS

9, rue du Pont Louis-Philippe
4th ARRONDISSEMENT ~ MÉTRO Saint-Paul
TÉLÉPHONE 01 42 77 70 49
Monday through Saturday ~ noon to 7pm
www.papierplus.com

———

I T SEEMS THAT OPPOSITES ATTRACT. DIRECTLY ACROSS FROM THE OLD WORLDLY BOUTIQUE MÉLODIES GRAPHIQUES IS THE ultra-modern Papier Plus, a stationery store that specializes in fresh, simple, and minimalist paper products. The two stores complement each other in their differences and regularly refer customers to each other when they don't have what the customer requires.

The Papier Plus boutique is stark and sparingly furnished, allowing the vibrant colors of the papers to pop. There is a vast range of colors to choose from, and with countless products covered in lovely textured monochromatic fabrics, you can easily color-code your entire office, from filing boxes to notepads, photo albums, portfolios, folders, and archival containers. There are even pencils to match. You'll also find colored sheets of paper available for computer printers, and an assortment of sleek accessories. The shop is popular with architects and photographers, who purchase portfolios to present their latest designs and images. Notebooks start at just under 20€ and escalate from there according to the size and function of the item.

WANDER

4

The Sixth Arrondissement

WANDER

WITH THE BUSTLING BOULEVARD ST-GERMAIN AND PLENTY OF LITTLE STREETS TO GET LOST AND FOUND IN, THIS QUARTER IS A PART of Paris where artisans and artists have always flourished. Today, even with the extravagant costs of commercial spaces in the area, there are still a number of wonderful *fait main* treasure chests to be unlocked.

cate handcrafted pieces.

The business started from a simple, albeit sexy, idea. Inspired by the way an earring dangles to catch the light on a woman's bare neck, or a bracelet accentuates a delicate inner wrist, Martell wanted to create a piece of jewelry that could be clipped to lingerie to embellish other parts of the body. And so was born *l'attachante*—a charm-inspired drop encrusted with jewels and silver motifs. There is a line for men as well, creations that can be clipped onto suit jackets to replace the old-fashioned *boutonnière*. Stéphan comes from a family of diamond jewelers, and his background heavily influences his flawless craftsmanship. The pieces range from 40€ to 1200€, with the average price about 150€.

SIMONE D'AVRAY

14, rue de l'Echaudé
6th ARRONDISSEMENT ~ MÉTRO Mabillon
TÉLÉPHONE 01 44 07 11 69
Tuesday through Saturday ~ noon to 7pm

A GLASS CABINET ON THE FAÇADE OF A BUILDING IN ONE OF ST-GERMAIN-DES-PRÉS' POSH BACK STREETS IS ALL the space jeweler Simone d'Avray needs to display her latest creations. Perched on a crimson-colored wall framed in apple green, the *vitrine* serves as the boutique, housing a beautiful collection of jewelry crafted by Madame d'Avray.

Her *atelier*, too, is on the premises—to the right of the cabinet is a doorway that leads into a two-square-meter entrance-way that leads nowhere. Enclosed in this tiny space Madame d'Avray works on her pieces—hammering, twisting, clipping, and joining minute fragments of metal to create spectacular adornments. Her style is diverse—she follows no patterns or drawings, creating as she goes—and her range is vast. In her cabinet are ultra-modern matte silver earrings and simple necklace bands alongside lavish gold designs threaded with shells and crystal beading. There are traditional brooch designs made into necklaces enhanced with matching glass pearls, and large round polished-stone rings. She also showcases items by other local jewelers and works with a few designer friends to create one-off pieces for her boutique.

at the ceiling, giving shoppers the feeling of standing under one of the shop's extravagant parasols.

Madame Sojfer's imagination is limitless when it comes to her umbrellas. Upon opening one of her seemingly simple canopies you will find tiny diamantes attached to the inside, so that as you walk the drops cast beautiful reflections into the framework. There are tassels dangling from the frames of some, and oversized fabric floral creations on others. Prices start at 155€.

Marie Mercié Paris London

GEORGES DE PROVIDENCE

3, rue de Fleurus
6th ARRONDISSEMENT ~ MÉTRO St-Placide
TÉLÉPHONE 01 42 84 48 79
Monday through Saturday • 11am to 7pm ~ CLOSED August
www.georgesdeprovidence.com

FAIRLY NEW ON THIS BLOCK IS THE HIGHLY FASHIONABLE ESTABLISHMENT GEORGES DE PROVIDENCE, CREATED BY interior designers Eric Foussat and Laurent Chwast. Situated between the trendy Bread and Roses café and the Jardin du Luxembourg, it's a lovely place to wander into for a *fait main* fix.

Foussat and Chwast design a range of streamlined, industrial-style furniture and also rework otherwise abandoned pieces, such as metal school chairs and oversized floor lamps. Natural light spills through the front windows and illuminates the store's stylish mix of wares, which combine sleek retro with a quirky edge. An element of street art lingers in the two show-rooms, which also showcase clothing—black cloud cut-outs have been fashioned into clothing racks that appear to have been inspired by a vintage comic book. They add a whimsical, dreamy feel to the white space, and fabulously show off the hip selection of clothing from various European designers, including the collection of French electro band Daft Punk. Eric Foussat's wife also designs and makes garments, reinter-preting vintage clothing into ultra-chic outfits. Her feminine and classy silk scarf dresses run 180€ to 580€.

georges de providence

GÉRALDINE VALLUET

5, rue Houdon

18th ARRONDISSEMENT ~ MÉTRO Pigalle

TÉLÉPHONE 01 42 52 29 63

Tuesday through Saturday ~ 10am to 8pm, Sunday and Monday ~ 2 to 8pm

http://www.atelier-geraldine-valluet-paris.com

P AINTED A VIBRANT TURQUOISE WITH HOT-PINK FEATHER-LINED WINDOW DISPLAYS, THE EXTERIOR OF THIS CHIC *atelier*-boutique perfectly emulates this designer's feminine, playful style. Open the door, enter the room behind the frosted window, and step into Géraldine Valluet's personal jewelry box.

Born in Paris, Valluet has been making jewelry for the haute couture catwalks since the early nineties; she opened her *atelier*-boutique here on rue Houdon in 2003. With a fluffy cloud skyscape floor, this boutique is *très* plush: decked out in luxurious velvet, seventeenth century–style glass display cabinets, and ornate gilded mirrors; awash with romantic colors like lilac, plum, crimson, and sapphire blue . . . could it be that you are standing in Marie Antoinette's personal dressing room?

Valluet has four main lines of jewelry: the delicate *fantaisie* range, with items starting at around 25€ and working up to 500€; the gold *précieux* collection; the special gold-chained *chérubin* range for little girls; and the haute couture *argent* range, with stunning semiprecious stones that dangle like charms. In addition, there is the bohemian range for men

that includes cufflinks inlaid with Swarvowski crystals.

Every one of the designs is handmade on the premises. She loves to experiment with mixed materials, combining rare jewels and delicate silver chains with glass, feathers, and tiny polished stones fashioned into butterfly and floral motifs. She is also happy to make jewelry *sur mesure*, so be sure to bring along your sketches and ideas when you stop by.

MAISON CLAIRVOY

Nowadays, with these young lads newly in charge, Maison Clairvoy is back to accepting orders from those among the general public who want something extra special in their shoe collection. Although getting shoes *sur mesure* doesn't come cheap, with orders starting at around 500€, you can be sure that your unique handcrafted heels will be exceptional, fit for any impromptu red carpet appearance.

This is a must-see when you are in the vicinity of the Moulin Rouge. Even if you don't walk into this seemingly insignificant storefront to see the old theatre posters and gaze at the latest creations being shaped and fitted, you can admire the weird and wonderful shoe collection displayed in the front window.

GALERIE ART KRAFT

28, rue Chaptal
9th ARRONDISSEMENT ~ MÉTRO Blanche
TÉLÉPHONE 06 60 44 82 35
Call for hours

T HE INDUSTRIAL AGE OF THE EARLY TWENTIETH CEN-TURY THAT BROUGHT MASS-PRODUCED GOODS QUICKLY resulted in a surplus of these same goods, which would be discarded to make room for the next "new and better" mass-produced item.

These century-old industrial scraps, especially highly functional metal furnishings, caught the interest of three Parisian artisans who started Art Kraft in 1993 based on their shared passion for creating sculpture and innovative functional furniture out of found metals and raw woods. They are inspired by their scrap finds but they also work with new materials—they'll use whatever it takes to re-create the pieces they envision.

The clever results of their labors are displayed and sold in this warehouse-style showroom, opened in 2000, in the artsy and not-very-touristy ninth *arrondissement*. Prices range from 200€ for a small lamp to 1500€ for a one-of-a-kind freestanding light fixture and around 1800€ for sculptures and large furniture such as tables and lounge chairs.

Some of the most striking creations are fan heads cleverly

reworked into sconces that cast eye-catching shadows against the red-painted walls. A coil of industrial globes forms a stunning wall feature, and the rusty metal castle tower on wheels captures the imagination. Each handcrafted object looks to have its own vibrant personality, evoking thoughts that perhaps when night falls and everyone is sound asleep, this room full of rusty relics just might come to life.

GALERIE VÉGÉTALE

29, rue des Vinaigriers
10th ARRONDISSEMENT ~ MÉTRO Château d'Eau
TÉLÉPHONE 01 40 37 07 16
Tuesday through Thursday, and Sunday • 10:30am to 7pm,
Friday and Saturday • 10:30am to 8pm

ALERIE VÉGÉTALE IS A GALLERY AND AN *ATELIER* WHERE DESIGN AND NATURE MEET TO PLAY, CONVERSE, AND create magic. What was formerly a warehouse has been invaded by nature. The founding partners—one an architect, the other an historian, both with a love of vegetation and art—decided to make a business out of their shared passions and set up shop in this industrial space, keeping the stark, grotty structure, and encouraging nature to run wild.

Two rooms are dedicated to exhibitions and a third is used as a florist *atelier*. There are succulents in tiny metal pots, handmade papers from unusual plant fibers (a favorite of mine for unique gift wrap), bamboo sculptures, and hand-crafted fountains and ponds. The team makess everything from traditional floral arrangements to large-scale floral sculptures of exotic flora like mini willows, blue ferns, and carnivorous plants. Not only do I come here for unique arrangements for my photo shoots, but for bursts of inspiration provided by the monthly art exhibitions.

CRISTALLERIE SCHWEITZER

84, Quai de Jemmapes

10th ARRONDISSEMENT ~ MÉTRO Château d'Eau

TÉLÉPHONE 01 42 39 61 63

Monday through Friday • 9am to noon and 2 to 5pm, or by appointment

THIS UNASSUMING WAREHOUSE—ACCESSIBLE ONLY THROUGH THE HUGE, TYPICALLY PARISIAN WOODEN DOORS THAT lead into a seemingly private courtyard—is a hidden *fait main* gem where Parisians have their chandeliers, crystal vases, and candelabras repaired.

Positioned just opposite Canal Saint Martin, Cristallerie is buzzing with activity. The staff claims to have repaired every type of glass and crystal on earth. And the word "repairing" is not used lightly on these premises, for repairing can mean reproducing a broken piece entirely from scratch. After the blowing work is done elsewhere, the rough piece is brought to the *atelier* and refined to make an identical match to the damaged original. With its 120-year-old machinery and tools, the *atelier* is like a step back in time. The polishing is done using pieces of cork, a technique dating back to the fourteenth century. Acid—commonly used by modern crystal repairers—is not used here.

A little room adjacent to main *atelier* is filled with glass and crystal pieces that were discarded or deserted but are now in mint condition and available for purchase. Prices depend on the complexity of the pieces and the time spent making the

repairs. Even if you are not interested in having a piece of crystal repaired while in Paris, you must stop by for a peek— the manager is welcoming and just happens to be a wonderfully entertaining tour guide.

comic strip "Tintin.") There is another larger *atelier* just outside Paris where a team of ten works on orders from around the world.

MALHIA KENT

19, avenue Daumesnil
12th ARRONDISSEMENT ~ MÉTRO Bastille
TÉLÉPHONE 01 53 44 76 76
Monday through Saturday + noon to 7pm
www.malhia.fr

THE FAÇADE OF THIS DAUMESNIL STUDIO REVEALS LITTLE. A HAND-LETTERED CARDBOARD SIGN PROPPED IN THE window indicates the name of the shop only, and the large arched windows reflect so much sunlight that it's difficult to see what is going on behind the glass. But don't leave—what lurks inside is so fabulous you will be pinching yourself in disbelief the moment you step inside.

This is the *atelier* of Malhia Kent. If you're not in the fashion industry, you may not realize the significance of the name. But perhaps the names Chanel, Yves Saint Laurent, Christian Dior, Christian Lacroix, and Armani ring a bell. Malhia Kent is connected to each of them in a very close way.

Enough with the mystery: Malhia Kent has created custom-made textiles for the *haute couture maisons* since founder Michèle Sorano first bought a loom in 1961. Although she died in 1998, her designs and studio continue under the company's new owner, the former model Eve Korrigan.

Run your fingers over the woven fabrics that adorn the front of the *atelier* to feel the exquisite hand. Luxurious silk ribbons are interwoven with a plethora of fibers and yarns,

creating a stunning series of tweed textiles. The wooden looms in the front room, bathed in sunlight, appear to be weaving sunbeams alongside the silk strands.

Although a shopper who wanders in off the street might at first feel she is not meant to be in here, that's not the case. There are scarves, coats made with leftover wovens, and small yardages of cloth for sale, and the general public is welcome. With prices starting at only 15€, this is a slice of *haute couture* fashion that you will never find anywhere else.

ATELIERS ROBIN TOURENNE

71, avenue Daumesnil
12ᵗʰ ARRONDISSEMENT ~ MÉTRO Bastille
TÉLÉPHONE 01 43 07 59 25
Monday through Saturday ~ 11am to 7pm
www.ateliers-robin-tourenne.com

NOTHER PLACE FREQUENTED BY PARISIAN DESIGNERS AND DECORATORS IS ATELIERS ROBIN TOURENNE, NOTED restorer of paper art.

Twenty-five years ago, when owner Robin Tourenne was a theatrical director, he discovered that old cinema and theater posters were becoming highly collectible but, unfortunately, often deteriorated rapidly. Teaching himself through books and hands-on experience, he began learning to restore them. The project soon turned into a business, and he now employs a skilled team of six, including two apprentices.

The *atelier* is a hive of activity, with customers coming in for restoration work on their vintage Henri Toulouse-Lautrec posters, and the apprentices busy preparing canvas backings and checking over antique gilded frames. The shelves are packed with old maps, wallpapers from the nineteenth century, and art nouveau *affiches*, all awaiting the specialized services of Tourenne and his team.

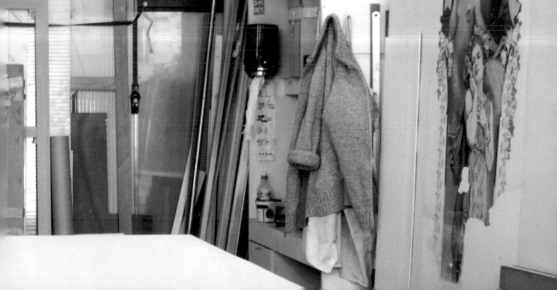

The workshop is concealed beneath the showroom so you won't be able to see the chandeliers being made, but it's nice to know that such exquisiteness is being fashioned by hand right on the premises, using traditional techniques and the antique designs constructed from bronze, gold, iron, and crystal. One of Baguès' most sought-after iconic designs is the dazzling parrot; a single wall sconce is priced at around 500€. The golden unicorn crystal ship hanging in the front window, designed in 1932, will surely leave a deep impression on you as you stroll back out into the real world. This is the stuff dreams are made of.

After you have strolled along the *promenade plantée* (garden path) that leads you back along the bridge over avenue Daumesnil, take a detour to the animated strip of rue du Faubourg Saint Antoine. True, is it crammed with expensive houseware stores, but it is also home to one of the gems of this city's arts and crafts community (see below).

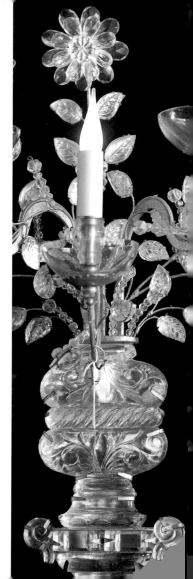

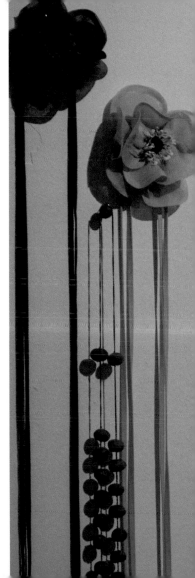

ATELIERS DE PARIS

30 rue du Faubourg St-Antoine
12th ARRONDISSEMENT ~ MÉTRO Bastille
TÉLÉPHONE 01 44 73 83 50
Monday through Friday ~ 9am to 1pm and 2 to 6pm
www.paris.fr/portail/Economie/Portal.lut?page_id=5886

THE ATELIERS DE PARIS IS COMPLETELY FUNDED BY THE CITY OF PARIS. WITH SIX STUDIOS IN THE FOUR-STORY structure, the association houses artisans in the fields of design, fashion, and all *métiers d'art* (jewelers, sculptors, metalworkers, woodworkers, and so on). The selected artisans are given a six-month renewable contract to practice their craft in their designated studios, and the association provides a gallery on the ground floor in which their works can be viewed and purchased by the public.

The gallery is a fascinating space to walk through. Among the artists in residence recently were young French jewelry designer Camille Lescure, whose Jungle Jungle collection is fashioned from fishbone and glass beads. There is no doubt that her pieces are destined for the *haute couture* catwalks. Another recent artist in residence was D.O.M.I., a textile and design duo who have fashioned incredibly alluring housewares and furniture from the very humble, utilitarian rubber band. Mosaic artist Solène Léglise is another star resident, having participated in the restoration of the historical mosaic monuments of the Petit Palais, the Vivienne Gallery, and La Grande Mosquée de Paris.

J'apprends à dessiner les Animaux

ATELIER D'ART DE FRANCE BOUTIQUES

22-26, avenue Niel
17th ARRONDISSEMENT ~ MÉTRO Ternes
TÉLÉPHONE 01 48 88 06 58
Tuesday through Saturday • 11am to 7pm
www.atelierdart.com

THE NOT-TO-BE-MISSED BOUTIQUE SPACES OF THE ATELIERS D'ART DE FRANCE ARE A LEISURELY WALK FROM THE bustling Place de l'Etoile. Co-owner of the well-known Maison & Object fair, the 140-year-old Ateliers d'Art de France is part of the French Federation for Craft Professionals. These three adjoining boutiques are ever-changing spaces for the work of the thirteen hundred crafts-people of the association, with one shop dedicated to hand-crafted furniture and sculpture, another to jewelry, and the third to ceramics and glassware—all unique, all handmade, and all French.

The selection is carefully curated to ensure that customers find that special *je ne sais quoi*. In the jewelry boutique you might find funky feather hoop earrings teamed with a 1920s-inspired woolen ladies' cap; a pearl and wood choker may share the same display cabinet as a tribal-style neck piece woven with wooden beads, buttons, and exotic feathers. There are shiny ceramic bead necklaces that appear to have been inspired by Paris' famous *macarons*, and necklaces, made from tiny glass marblelike beads, wrapped intricately in thread

and linked to form long chains to adorn your waist or neck.

The furniture boutique is a melange of classical bronze sculptures, Asian-influenced light fixtures, and impeccably crafted freestanding clocks made in Besançon in eastern France. In the tabletop shop you will find Venetian-style designs among the glassware, as well as modern, simple vessels and decorative housewares.

It's obvious that creativity thrives in these spaces: the changing displays are works of art in themselves. A recent installation used unusual succulents and exotic flora to display the handmade goods. An enthusiastic and knowledgeable staff manages the boutiques, and the service is outstanding.

galerie d'objets

L'ANGE
en chair et en o...

WANDER

9

The Eighteenth Arrondissement

WANDER

STROLLING THROUGH MONTMARTRE ON A SUNNY SPRING DAY IS A MOST ENJOYABLE PARISIAN EXPERIENCE, WITH THE MOULIN ROUGE, Sacre Coeur, and the Manège de Montmartre (Montmartre carousel) to wander between. But adding some hidden-away, treasure-filled *fait main* boutiques and *ateliers* to that sunny stroll through Montmartre is simply heavenly.

TOMBÉES DU CAMION

17, rue Joseph de Maistre
18ᵗʰ ARRONDISSEMENT ~ MÉTRO Abbesses or Blanche
TÉLÉPHONE 01 77 15 05 02
Monday through Friday ∗ 1 to 8pm, Saturday and Sunday ∗ 11am to 8pm
www.tombeesducamion.com

BEFORE YOU HEAD UP THE SECOND HILL OF RUE LEPIC (WHEN COMING FROM METRO BLANCHE) WANDER A LITTLE past the fabulous fork-in-the-road, ivy-covered restaurant named Basilic to find Charles Mas' tiny boutique on your left. *Tombées du camion* literally translates as "goods fallen off the back of a truck." This is the fascinating concept behind this professional chineur's original shop. Tombées du Camion in a treasure chest, and it is about the size of one too, packed, in an ever-so orderly way, with the most eclectic of decades-old (but brand new) treasures: the items are all from a bygone era but are still in their original packaging or original state. Tiny dice and old wooden domino sets from the 1970s sit next to massive spools of beaded ribbon and old type from the 1940s, little doll bodies from the 1950s, and glass tubes from the 1930s. I have found many a prop for my photo shoots there. The window displays change weekly—one day fabric flowers and vintage scissors, the next painted baby boots and retro billiard balls. Prices range up to 100€, but the majority of items sell for 1€ to 15€, making it a bowerbird's heaven; you are sure to find plenty you will want to take home to your own nest.

Française. The Hotel du Louvre, across the street from the theatre, spotted her luminescent creations and ordered ten. It's hard to resist the urge to fit every hanging bulb and unlit corner of your home with an Estelle Lemaître-designed fixture.

The shades are combined with striking found objects that Madame Lemaître has turned into lamp bases. Plump glass jars, chunky wooden blocks, and rustic metal tins are among the collection, as well as more traditional ceramic and bronze bases. Prices range from 70€ to 900€. Also inside the shop are handmade creations from local artisans, including mirrors embellished with shells made by Estelle's sister, and bronze pieces made by Le Petit Parisien.

THIERRY LEFÉVRE-GRAVE

24, rue Durantin

18th ARRONDISSEMENT ~ MÉTRO Abbesses

TÉLÉPHONE 01 42 23 65 60

Tuesday through Saturday • 11am to 1pm and 3 to 7pm

THIERRY LEFÉVRE GRAVE HAS BEEN IN HIS *ATELIER*-BOU-
TIQUE ON RUE DURANTIN FOR OVER THIRTY YEARS,
having snapped up the grottolike street frontage back
when Montmartre was cheap and not so fashionable. Now
that it is one of the hippest *arrondissements* in the city,
Thierry's sculptures and jewelry can no longer be kept a
secret, even in the hush-hush world of Paris art collectors.

Lefévre-Grave works with all sorts of materials, including
marble, silver, bronze, and wood, and during his long career
as an artist he has become an expert in everything he puts
his hands to. You can linger outside the storefront standing
on tiptoes to try to get a glimpse of some of his pieces, or
push open the door and enter the workshop and take a good
look at what is on the workbench. Don't be shy; like all good
artisans, he is delighted for passersby to show interest in his
work.

Among an extraordinary collection of bronze sculptures of
whimsical longhaired ladies are the artist's unique glass and
silver rings and cufflinks (ranging from 200€ to 1000€ per
piece). His intricately designed silver pens are a recent cre-
ation and are made to order; they are his best sellers and are

often custom-made as gifts for hard-to-buy-for men. Starting at 850€, these crystal-point pens don't come cheap. Levévre-Grave's handiwork is pricey and contrasts greatly with his unpretentious workshop and showroom, but all for good reason. The superb craftsmanship is evident the moment you lay your eyes and hands on his pieces.

YONOIL

28, rue Durantin
18th ARRONDISSEMENT ~ MÉTRO Abbesses
TÉLÉPHONE 06 10 08 43 66
Tuesday through Friday + 3 to 7pm, Saturday and Sunday + 3 to 8pm

B Y NOW YOU'VE NOTICED THAT MANY OF PARIS' BUSY *ATELIERS* AND BOUTIQUES FILLED WITH HANDMADE treasures are unassuming, with seemingly insignificant exteriors, hidden in wisteria-framed passages or tucked away on quiet cobblestone alleys, Yonoil is no exception.

Just opposite Ebano you will spot the bright yellow façade of this dimly lit showroom filled with found treasures from bygone eras. Old Brilié and Lepaute wall clocks from closed-down factories and train stations adorn the walls (starting at 100€ each), while tallboy metal filing cabinets and rusted industrial desk lamps (starting at around 60€) from the 1950s clutter the floor space, giving you a sense of being in *grandpère's* attic. Virginie Souquière is the owner of this ever-changing, tasteful collection, and she reworks discarded items into highly desired housewares in the diminutive workshop behind the storefront. She also makes ceramics; prices range from just 8€ for bowls and plates to 150€ for her beautiful teapots.

Petites
Broches
€

LUNE

30, rue Durantin
18th ARRONDISSEMENT ~ MÉTRO Abbesses
TÉLÉPHONE 01 42 54 62 69
Tuesday through Sunday + 11:30am to 8:30pm
www.luneparis.com

LUNE IS A BOUTIQUE-*ATELIER* OVERFLOWING WITH FABULOUS FASHION ACCESSORIES FOR WOMEN CRAFTED FROM silk and satin men's ties. Young Swiss-turned-Parisienne designer Céline Jendly opened the shop in 2003. After ten years of working in the fashion world, she wanted to have her own space in which to work in a more hands-on way. She came up with the idea of embellishing and reworking vintage men's ties as her signature concept, which she calls *prêt à cravater* (ready to tie).

Madame Jendly fabricates all sorts of remarkable pieces from tossed-away ties including sassy hats, belts, brooches, necklaces, and wristbands. And there are some ties, too, embellished with bright retro buttons, colorful ribbons, and fabric flowers. The store is a candyland of handmade booty displayed on tables from the sixties and marble-topped dressers, with garments hanging from antique gilded mirrors and old dressmaker forms. The boutique is lit with opulent chandeliers and twinkling fairy lights. Peek around the corner of the back wall and you will find the designer and her assistants busy at work in the studio, stitching and weaving the ties into fanciful creations.

Alongside the *prêt à cravater* range is the *prêt à chiner* line of restyled vintage clothing that Madame Jendly sources in *brocantes*, and the *prêt à rêver* (ready to dream) collection, which is a selection of garments made for clients with more classic taste. Prices range from 20€ to 350€.

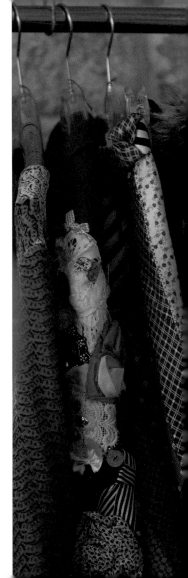

OFF THE BEATEN TRACK

The Eleventh & Twelfth Arrondissements

ATELIER FI.É
- 201 -

ATELIER 154
- 205 -

ATELIER BEAU TRAVAIL
- 209 -

OFF THE BEATEN TRACK

P ARIS IS A BIG CITY, AND NOT ALL DESTINATIONS ARE WITHIN WAN-
DERING DISTANCE FROM ONE ANOTHER. HERE IS A *PETIT MÉLANGE*
of some of the loveliest ateliers around town and off the beaten
track, each well worth the extra *métro* stop or two.

ATELIER FLÉ

Passage du 26, rue de Charonne
11th ARRONDISSEMENT ~ MÉTRO Ledru Rollin
TÉLÉPHONE 01 47 00 81 22
Open by appointment

R ARELY THESE DAYS DO YOU GET AN OPPORTUNITY TO WANDER INTO THE SECLUDED COBBLESTONE COURTYARDS of Paris. Once filled with workshops bustling with artisans and tradesfolk, they are now mostly private, for residents only. But they are ever so intriguing, especially when one of the huge wooden doors is ajar, allowing a peek into a centuries-old *passage*, bursting with wisteria bathed in morning light.

After 180 years, the leatherworker Atelier Flé is still in business, tucked discreetly into one of these untouched walkways of old Paris. (Today there are only two artisans left here.) Once you cross the threshold and pass through the shadowy vestibule, it's hard not to get immersed in the atmosphere. Atelier Flé is all about atmosphere: the exterior is covered in rambling ivy that appears to be unchanged since its founding.

Current owner Marie-Jeanne Greenaway describes the almost-forgotten era when the furniture trades thrived in this area some two hundred years ago. Wood would be hauled up to the top floors of the buildings via ropes, and then journey down through the various *ateliers*. In each workshop a craftsman specializing in some now-lost skill would add his labor to produce an exquisite piece of furniture. By the time a piece had worked its way to the ground floor, Atelier Flé would be ready to add the final touches of leatherwork and gilding to the masterpiece.

Madame Greenaway works tirelessly on incoming orders, mostly restoration work for the *mobilier national* (the governmental department for state-owned antique furniture). In addition, she works on both restoration projects and new furniture requiring leather upholstery for international interior designers and private individuals. She is also one of the last remaining artisans in the area who can dye leather, using tools that date back to the eighteenth century. Her skill is one that can be learned only by practice. Even if you have no interest in having a piece of furniture imprinted with gold in a Louis XVI design, this *atelier* is not to be missed for its sheer historic value.

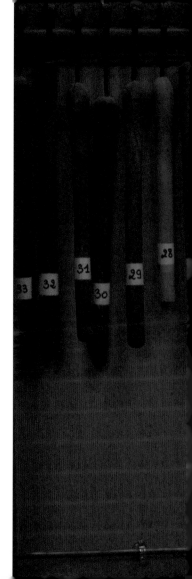

ATELIER 154

154, rue Oberkampf
11ᵗʰ ARRONDISSEMENT ~ MÉTRO Ménilmontant or Parmentier
TÉLÉPHONE 06 62 32 79 06
Thursday through Saturday ~ 2 to 7pm
www.atelier154.com

—

ATELIER 154 IS SET AT THE END OF A LONG COBBLESTONE OPENING BETWEEN TWO EDIFICES. (NOTE: LEARN FROM MY mistakes and leave your high heels at home for this one.) The sad news is that the new landowner is requesting that all the *ateliers* and galleries move out to make room for new development, endangering the survival of this wonderfully occluded lane of *fait main* wares.

However, Stéphane Quatresous, the proprietor and artisan of Atelier 154, is not so willing to budge, and has recently secured a second showroom in the *passage*. While his first *atelier*, at the back of the lane, is desirably dim and cavelike, with an incredible selection of reworked industrial treasures, the new *atelier*, found midway up the passage, is light, bright, and mostly white. Both spaces embody Quatresous's concept of reworking old industrial pieces into functional, modern, and very stylish home furniture. There are fifties Jielde lamps, Bienaise and Flambo work chairs, twenties postal desks and adjustable drafting tables, plus the more common *brocante* finds, like old Paris street signs and rusted metal letters. Quatresous has such an eye for style that even the most pedestrian items in his showrooms are

superbly refashioned and exhibited. He has started collect-
ing fabulous vintage plastic ensembles in bold cherry red
and combining them with more pallid pieces. When he finds
industrial pieces he likes, he buys and reworks only a few, to
guarantee their exclusive nature—which does come at a
price. His tables can start at around 1200€.

ATELIER BEAU TRAVAIL

67, rue de la Mare
20ᵗʰ ARRONDISSEMENT ~ MÉTRO Jourdain
NO TÉLÉPHONE
Saturdays - 2:30 to 7:30pm or by appointment
www.beautravail.fr/blog

A LITTLE BIT OF A TREK FROM THE MAIN STREETS OF PARIS BUT WELL WORTH THE JOURNEY ON A SATURDAY AFTER-noon, Atelier Beau Travail was founded by four Parisian artisans with a passion for *bricoler*. Each has her own items displayed in the store: Delphine Dunoyer makes cheerful handbags with a retro twist, under the label Aconit Napel; Céline Saby fashions block lampshades from bold Japanese cloth; Séverine Balanqueux makes adorable children's clothes from soft cottons, light linens, and other natural fab-rics; and Caroline Halusiak is the woman behind the well-known "ah, quel plaisir!" collection of handmade housewares.

The studio-boutique offers a wonderful mix and is calm and inviting, with tons of treats to suit all handmade tastes. Along with the four designers' collections, another fifteen to twenty collections from French and European designers are rotated throughout the year. Every two to three months the four original artisans organize a three-day exhibition to present the new designers. The wares are also sold interna-tionally on line.

ABOUT THE AUTHOR

Pia Jane Bijkerk is an Australian stylist and photographer specializing in still life, food, interiors, and lifestyle imagery. She has a special interest in forecasting design trends. She lives in Amsterdam and Paris, and works internationally for magazines and advertising agencies. Clients include *Vogue Entertaining & Travel*, *Real Simple*, *Marie Claire*, and Saatchi & Saatchi. Her work can be seen at piajanebijkerk.com.

INDEX

Fifty shops where decorators, designers, and stylists source the chic & unique.

PARISIAN DESIGNERS ARE ENCHANTED BY ALL THINGS *FAIT MAIN*, OR "MADE BY HAND." STYLIST PIA BIJKERK LEADS YOU TO MORE THAN 50 SHOPS AND STUDIOS THAT embody that spirit and where you'll find the most original and creative clothing, jewelry, handbags, ceramics, home furnishings, and decorative objects in Paris.

US $18.95   CAN $22.00   UK £12.99
ISBN 978-1-892145-70-3

5 1 8 9 5
9 781892 145703

THE LITTLE BOOKROOM
New York